Wee Sing®

BIBLE SONGS

by
Pamela Conn Beall and
Susan Hagen Nipp

Illustrated by
Nancy Spence Klein

PRICE STERN SLOAN
Los Angeles

To Life

Special thanks to our Wee Singers: Hilary Beall, Kyle
Beall, Lindsay Beall, Ryan Nipp, Devin Nipp, Sam Klein,
Erin Klein, Katie Klein, Rachel Macy,
Peter Macy and John Macy....

And to our musical producers
Barry Hagen and Mauri Macy

Printed on recycled paper

Cover Illustration by Dennis Hockerman

Copyright © 1986 by Pamela Conn Beall and Susan Hagen Nipp
Published by Price Stern Sloan, Inc.
A member of The Putnam & Grosset Group, New York, New York.

ISBN: 0-8431-1566-1

PSS!® and Wee Sing® are registered trademarks of Price Stern Sloan, Inc.

24 23 22 21 20

PREFACE

Sing unto God, sing praises to His name
Psalm 68:4
I will sing praises unto the Lord
Psalm 27:6

Just as David in the Psalms writes of singing praises to God, we continue to sing of God's glory in our contemporary world.

In *Wee Sing Bible Songs,* we have collected mainly traditional songs of unknown origin that children have loved for years. They tell of Bible heroes, teachings, parables, praises and prayers with many of their lyrics being directly related to specific passages of the Bible. We have noted these Scripture verses above the music so you can refer to them and more fully understand the background of the song.

A selection of spirituals has been omitted because we previously published them in *Wee Sing Around the Campfire.* In that book you will find "Oh When the Saints," "Joshua Fought the Battle," "Get on Board Little Children," "Heav'n, Heav'n," "Nobody Knows the Trouble I've Seen," "Jacob's Ladder," "Swing Low," "Rocka My Soul," "One More River" and the full story of "Rise and Shine."

Whether you are memorizing the books of the Bible through song, singing the story of David and Goliath or lifting your voice in praise, we hope you enjoy the gift that God has given us all – – – – music.

Pam Beall
Susan Nipp

TABLE OF CONTENTS

The Bible Says

*Titles with asterisks are fingerplays which are rhymes illustrated by the use of finger motions.

We Praise and Pray

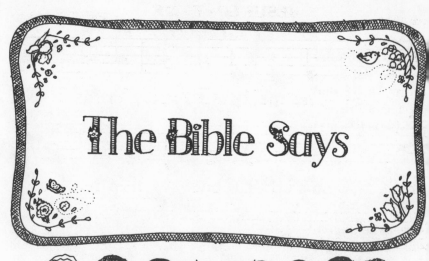

The Bible Says

JESUS LOVES THE LITTLE CHILDREN

C.H. Woolston

George F. Roo

Je-sus loves the lit-tle chil-dren,

All the chil-dren of the world, Red and

yel-low, black and white, They are pre-cious in His

sight, Je-sus loves the lit-tle chil-dren of the world.

JESUS LOVES ME

Wm. B. Bradbury

Je-sus loves me, this I know, For the Bi-ble

tells me so ; Lit-tle ones to Him be-long,

They are weak, but He is strong.

Chorus

Yes, Je-sus loves me, Yes, Je-sus loves me,

Yes, Je-sus loves me, The Bi-ble tells me so.

gn language

Jesus   loves   me   this   I   know

For   Bible   tells   me   so

Chorus:

Yes   Jesus loves me (3 times)
(see line 1)

Bible tells me so
(see line 2)

ittle ones   Him   belong

hey   weak   He   strong

7

JESUS LOVES EVEN ME

I am so glad that Je-sus loves me

Je-sus loves me, Je-sus loves me, I am so glad t

Je-sus loves me, Je-sus loves e-ven me.

*Guitar play in key of E (E, A, B7)

JESUS SEES ME

Jesus sees me when I sleep,
  (rest head on hands)

Jesus sees me when I play,
  (turn around)

Jesus sees me all the time,
  (arms outstretched)

And he cares for me each day.
  (cross arms over chest)

Suggestion:
Can be sung to the tune "Jesus Loves Me"

COME BLESS THE LORD

salm 134:1,2

Come bless the Lord, (Come bless the Lord,) all ye

ser-vants of the Lord, (all ye ser-vants of the

Lord,) who stand by night (who stand by night) in the

house of the Lord, (in the house of the Lord,) Lift

up your hands (Lift up your hands) in the

ho-ly place, (in the ho-ly place,) And

bless the Lord, (And bless the Lord) and

bless the Lord. (and bless the Lord.)

9

JESUS WANTS ME FOR A SUNBEAM

Nellie Talbot
Matthew 5:16

E.O. Exce...

Je-sus wants me for a sun-beam, To shine for Him each day, In ev'ry way try to please Him, At home, at school, at play.

Chorus

A sun-beam, a sun-beam, Je-sus wants me for a sun-beam, A sun-beam, a sun-beam, I'll be a sun-beam for Him.—

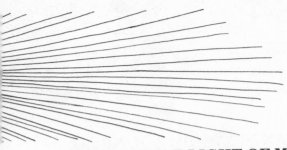

THIS LITTLE LIGHT OF MINE

Matthew 5:15-16

1. This lit-tle light of mine, I'm gon-na let it shine, This lit-tle light of mine, I'm gon-na let it shine, let it

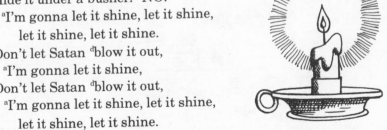

shine, let it shine, let it shine.

2. [b]Hide it under a bushel? [c]NO!
   [a]I'm gonna let it shine.
   [b]Hide it under a bushel? [c]NO!
   [a]I'm gonna let it shine, let it shine,
   let it shine, let it shine.

3. [a]Don't let Satan [d]blow it out,
   [a]I'm gonna let it shine,
   [a]Don't let Satan [d]blow it out,
   [a]I'm gonna let it shine, let it shine,
   let it shine, let it shine.

4. Repeat verse 1

Actions:
a) hold up left forefinger throughout verse   b) cover finger with right palm   c) shout "NO" and uncover finger   d) blow at top of finger instead of singing "blow"

THE BIBLE SAYS

The Bible says that Jesus
(hands form book)

Was loving, kind and good,
(cross arms on chest)

I want to live as Jesus did
(point to self)

And do the things I should.
(nod head)

THE LORD IS MY SHEPHERD
(Round)

Psalm 23

The Lord is my — shep-herd, I'll walk with Him al-way

He knows me and He loves me, I'll walk with Him al-way

Al-way, al-way, I'll walk with Him al-way.

Al-way, al-way, I'll walk with Him al-way.

DEEP AND WIDE

Psalm 36:9

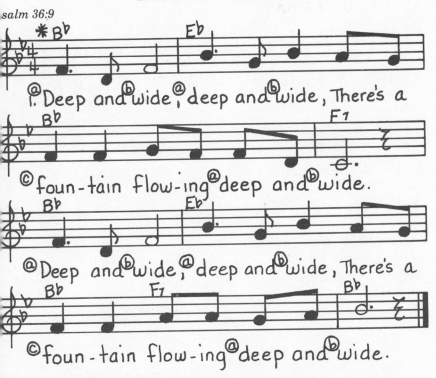

1. Deep and wide, deep and wide, There's a foun-tain flow-ing deep and wide. Deep and wide, deep and wide, There's a foun-tain flow-ing deep and wide.

2. Repeat song leaving out "deep" but do action
3. Repeat song leaving out "deep" and "wide" but do actions
4. Repeat song leaving out "deep," "wide" and "fountain," but do actions

Actions:
a) hands measure deep
b) hands measure wide
c) wiggle fingers left to right

* Guitar play in key of A (A, D, E⁷)

GOD MADE ME

1. @God made ⓑme, @God made ⓑme,
ⓒIn my Bi-ble-Book it says that @God made ⓑme.

2. ªGod loves ᵇme, ªGod loves ᵇme,
ᶜIn my Bible Book it says that
ªGod loves ᵇme.
3. ªGod helps ᵇme...
4. ªGod keeps ᵇme...

Actions:
a) point up   b) point to self
c) hands form book

MY BODY, STRONG AND GOOD

I have two eyes that wink and blink,
  I have a mind to make me think,
I have two hands that clap for fun,
  I have two feet that jump and run,
I have two ears to hear a song,
  Two lips to praise Him all day long,
I have a body strong and good,
  To use for Jesus as I should.

Actions:
Point to body parts and do as words suggest.

14

OH, BE CAREFUL
(Tune: If You're Happy)

1. Oh, be care-ful lit-tle eyes what you see,

Oh, be care-ful lit-tle eyes what you see,

For the Fa-ther up a-bove is look-ing down in love,

So be care-ful lit-tle eyes what you see.

Oh, be ^dcareful little ears what you hear,
  Oh, be ^dcareful little ears what you hear,
For the ^bFather up above is ^clooking down in love,
  So be ^dcareful little ears what you hear.
. Oh, be ^ecareful little hands what you do...
. Oh, be ^fcareful little feet where you go...
. Oh, be ^gcareful little heart whom you trust...
. Oh, be ^hcareful little mind what you think...

Actions:
) point to eyes   b) point up   c) shade eyes   d) cup hands around ears
 hold out hands   f) point to feet   g) hands over heart   h) point to temple

Guitar play in key of E (E, A, B⁷)

15

SILVER AND GOLD HAVE I NONE

Pe-ter and John went to pray;— They met a lame

man on the way, He asked for alms — and

held out his palms and this is what Pe-ter did

say:— "Sil-ver and gold have I none,— but

such as I have give I thee, In the name of

Je — sus Christ— of Naz-a-reth, rise up and

walk." He went walk-ing and leap-ing and

prais-ing God, walk-ing and leap-ing and

16

prais-ing God, "In the name of Je —— sus
Christ —— of Naz-a-reth, rise up and walk."

THE TWELVE DISCIPLES

Peter, Andrew, James and John,
   Fishermen of Capernaum,
Thomas and St. Matthew, too,
   Philip and Bartholomew,
James, his brother Thaddeus,
   Simon, and the one named Judas,
Twelve disciples here in all,
   Following the Master's call.

BEHOLD, BEHOLD

Revelations 3:20

Be-hold, be-hold! I stand at the door and

Knock, Knock, Knock; Be-hold, be-hold! I

stand at the door and knock, Knock, Knock; If

an-y-one hear my voice, If an-y-one hear my voic

and will o-pen, o-pen, o-pen the door, I will come in

Actions:
a) knock three times   b) right hand cup ear   c) left hand cup ear   d) hand
measure narrow   e) hands wider apart   f) hands even wider apart   g) hands ove
heart

WELCOME

* Guitar play in key of A (A, D, E, E⁷, B⁷)

18

ONE DOOR AND ONLY ONE

*F

One door and on-ly one, And yet its sides are two,

Bb   F   G   C7

In-side and out-side, On which side are you?

F

One door and on-ly one, And yet its sides are two,

Bb   F   C7   F

I'm on the in-side, On which side are you?

Actions:
a) hold up forefinger   b) hold up two fingers   c) hold up hand, palm facing in
d) palm facing out   e) point out   f) point to self

*Guitar play in key of E (E, A, B7, F)

LOVE, LOVE
(Round)

Leviticus 19:18

Em   D   Em   Bm   Em   D

Love, love, love, love, Chris-tians this

Em   Bm   Em   D

is your — call, Love your neigh-bor

Em   Bm   Em   D   Em

as your — self, For God loves — all.

19

THIS IS MY COMMANDMENT

John 15:12

This is my com-mand-ment that you love one an-oth-er, that your joy may be full. This is my com-mand-ment that you love one an-oth-er, that your joy may be full; That your joy may be full, That your joy may be full; This is my com-mand-ment that you love one an-oth-er that your joy may be full.

THE B-I-B-L-E

The B - I - B - L - E, yes, that's the
book for me, I @ stand a - lone on the
Word of God, The B - I - B - L - E.

Optional Descant

S.N.

The B-I-B-L-E, yes, that's the book for me, I
@ stand a - lone,— The B - I - B - L - E .

Action:
a) stand up

Suggestion:
Make a large card for each of the letters of B-I-B-L-E. Five children hold
the cards. As word is spelled, child holds letter above head. Hold in
front of chest for other lyrics.

BOOKS OF THE OLD TESTAMENT

Susan Nipp

Gen-e-sis, Ex-o-dus, Le-vi-ti-cus, Num-bers, Deu-ter-on-o-

my, Josh-ua, Judg-es, Ruth,— First and Se-cond Sam-ue

First Kings, Sec-ond Kings, First and Sec-ond Chron-i-cles,

Ez-ra, Ne-he-mi—ah, Es-ther, Job, Psalms, Pro—verbs, Ec

cle-si-as-tes, Song of Sol-o-mon, I-sai-ah, Jer-e-mi-ah

Lam-en-ta-tions, E-ze-kiel, Dan-iel, Ho-se-a, Joel, A-mos, O-ba-

di-ah, Jo-nah, Mi-cah, Na—hum, Ha-bak-kuk, Zeph-an-

i—ah, Hag-ga-i, Zech-a-ri-ah, and the last book Mal-a-chi

22

BOOKS OF THE NEW TESTAMENT

Susan Nipp

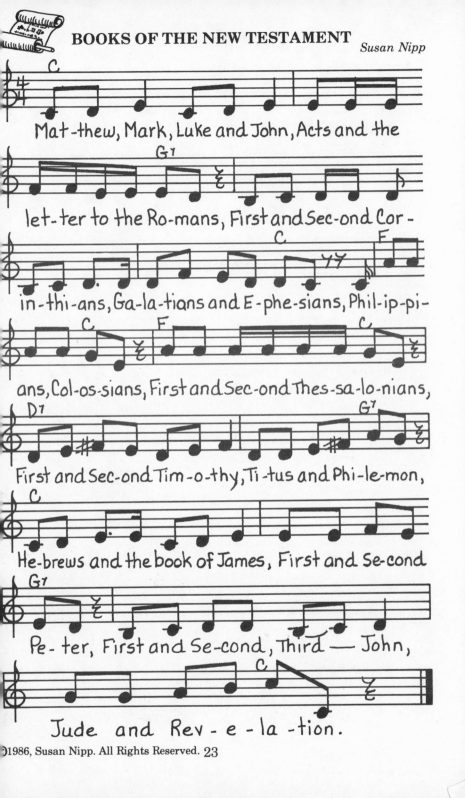

Mat-thew, Mark, Luke and John, Acts and the

let-ter to the Ro-mans, First and Sec-ond Cor -

in-thi-ans, Ga-la-tions and E-phe-sians, Phil-ip-pi-

ans, Col-os-sians, First and Sec-ond Thes-sa-lo-nians,

First and Sec-ond Tim-o-thy, Ti-tus and Phi-le-mon,

He-brews and the book of James, First and Se-cond

Pe-ter, First and Se-cond, Third — John,

Jude and Rev-e-la-tion.

1. Fa-ther Ab-ra-ham had man-y sons, man-y sons had Fa-ther Ab-ra-ham, I am one of the and so are you, so let's all praise the Lord. @Right ar

2. Father Abraham had many sons,
     Many sons had Father Abraham,
   I am one of them and so are you,
     So let's all praise the Lord.
   ªRight arm, ᵇleft arm!
3. Father Abraham...
     ªRight arm, ᵇleft arm, ᶜright foot!
4. ...ᵈleft foot!
5. ...ᵉchin up!
6. ...ᶠturn around!
7. ...ᵍsit down!

Actions:
a) clench fist, bend and extend arm upward repeatedly throughout song   b) add left arm in same motion as right   c) add right foot stepping up and down   d) add left foot stepping up and down   e) add head nodding up and down   f) add turning in place while continuing other motions   g) sit down

LITTLE DAVID, PLAY ON YOUR HARP

Spiritual

Lit-tle Da-vid play on your harp, Hal-le-lu, hal-le-lu, Lit-tle Da-vid play on your harp, Hal-le-lu.— Lit-tle Da-vid play on your harp, Hal-le-lu, hal-le-lu, Lit-tle Da-vid play on your harp, Hal-le-lu. ——

Lit-tle Da-vid was a shep-herd boy, He Killed Go-li-ath and shout-ed for joy. ——

ONLY A BOY NAMED DAVID

A.A.
I Samuel 17:49

Arthur Arnott

(h) in the sling, And the (b) sling went round and round;

And round and round and round and round, And

round and round and round, And (g) one lit-tle stone went

(i) up in the air, And the gi-ant came tum-bling down.

Actions:
a) hand in front, palm down as in measuring   b) circle hand above head   c) hands in prayer position   d) hands around mouth   e) wiggle fingers left to right   f) hold up five fingers   g) hold up forefinger   h) put finger into palm of opposite hand   i) shoot forefinger upward   j) fall down or clap

WHO DID SWALLOW JONAH?

1. Who did, who did, Who did, who did, Who did swal-low Jo, Jo, Jo, Jo, Who did, who did, Who did, who did, Who did swal-low Jo, Jo, Jo, Jo, Who did, who did, Who did, who did, Who did swal-low Jo, Jo, Jo, Jo, Who did swal-low Jo-nah, who did swal-low Jo-nah, Who did swal-low Jo-nah down? —

2. Whale did...swallow Jo, Jo, Jo, Jo... (3 times)
   Whale did swallow Jonah...down.
3. Gabriel...blow your trum, trum, trum, trum...
   Gabriel blow your trumpet...loud.
4. Noah...in the arky, arky...
   Noah in the arky...bailed.
5. Daniel...in the li, li, li, li...
   Daniel in the lion's...den.
6. Peter...on the sea, sea, sea, sea...
   Peter walking on the...sea.

28

ZACCHAEUS

Luke 19:1-5

Zac-chae-us was a wee lit-tle man, A wee lit-tle man was he, He climbed up in a sy-ca-more tree For the Lord he want-ed to see; And as the Sav-ior passed that way, He looked up in the tree, And He said: "Zac-chae-us, (spoken) you come down, For I'm go-ing to your house to-day, For I'm go-ing to your house to-day."

Actions:
a) hands in front, right palm raised above left palm as in measuring   b) palms
closer   c) alternate hands as if climbing   d) shade eyes, look down   e) swing
arms as in walking   f) shade eyes, look up   g) beckon with hand   h) clap in
rhythm

29

THE WISE MAN AND FOOLISH MAN

Matthew 7:24-27

1. The wise man built his house up - on the rock,

The wise man built his house up - on the rock,

The wise man built his house up - on the rock,

And the rains came tum - bling down.

Chorus

The rains came down and the floods came up,

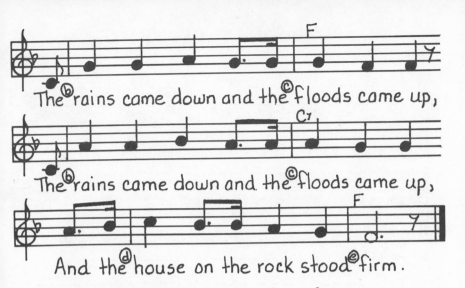

The ᵇrains came down and the ᶜfloods came up,

The ᵇrains came down and the ᶜfloods came up,

And the ᵈhouse on the rock stood ᵉfirm.

2. The ᶠfoolish man built his house upon the sand,
   The ᶠfoolish man built his house upon the sand,
   The ᶠfoolish man built his house upon the sand,
   And the ᵇrains came tumbling down.

Chorus:
   The ᵇrains came down and the ᶜfloods came up,
   The ᵇrains came down and the ᶜfloods came up,
   The ᵇrains came down and the ᶜfloods came up,
   And the ᵈhouse on the sand went ᵍSMASH!

Actions:
a) pound one fist on top of the other in rhythm   b) wiggle fingers while moving hands
downward   c) palms up, raise hands in rhythm   d) fingertips form rooftop
e) pound fists once   f) pound fist into open palm in rhythm   g) slap palms loudly

31

WHO BUILT THE ARK?

Genesis 6, 7

Spiritual

Chorus F Solo ... C7 Group

Who built the ark? No-ah! No-ah!

F Solo ... Group ... C7 ... F Fine

Who built the ark? Broth-er No-ah built the ark.

C. Solo

1. Old man No-ah built the ark, He built it out of the

G7 ... C

hick-o-ry bark. He built it long, both wide and tall

G7 ... C D.C.al Fine

With plen-ty of room for the large — and small.

2. In came the animals, two by two,
   Hippopotamus and kangaroo.
   In came the animals, three by three,
   Two big cats and a bumblebee.
   Chorus
3. In came the animals, four by four,
   Two through the window and two through the door.
   In came the animals, five by five,
   The bees came swarming from the hive.
   Chorus
4. In came the animals, six by six,
   Elephant laughed at the monkey's tricks.
   In came the animals, seven by seven,
   Giraffes and the camels looking up to heaven.
   Chorus
5. In came the animals, eight by eight,
   Some on time and the others were late.
   In came the animals, nine by nine,
   Some were laughin' and some were cryin'.
   Chorus
6. In came the animals, ten by ten,
   Time for the voyage to begin.
   Noah said, "Go shut the door,
   The rain's started fallin' and we can't take more."
   Chorus

33

HIS BANNER OVER ME IS LOVE

Song of Solomon 2:4, 16

2. He brought me to His banqueting table, ⎫ 3 times
      His banner over me is love... ⎭
   His banner over me is love.
3. He is the vine and we are the branches...
4. Jesus is the rock of my salvation...

Suggestion:

For younger children, use only verse 1 with these actions:

Actions:
a) point up   b) point to self   c) fingertips together over head   d) cross arms over chest

34

We Praise and Pray

PRAISE HIM, PRAISE HIM

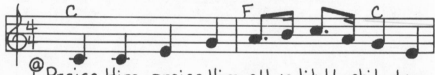

1. Praise Him, praise Him, all ye lit-tle chil-dren,

God is love, God is love, Praise Him, praise Him,

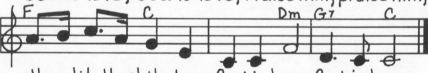

all ye lit-tle chil-dren, God is love, God is love.

2. [b]Love Him, love Him, all ye little children,
   God is love, God is love,
   Love Him, love Him, all ye little children,
   God is love, God is love.
3. [c]Thank Him, thank Him...
4. [d]Serve Him, serve Him...

Actions:
a) clap entire verse in rhythm   b) cross arms over chest   c) hands in prayer position   d) hands out front, palms up

35

KUM BA YAH
(Translation: Come By Here)

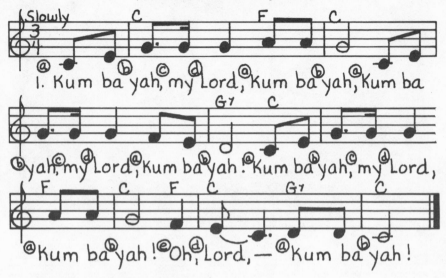

1. Kum ba yah, my Lord, Kum ba yah, Kum ba yah, my Lord, Kum ba yah! Kum ba yah, my Lord, Kum ba yah! Oh, Lord, — Kum ba yah!

2. ^fSomeone's crying, ^dLord, ^aKum ba ^byah,

3. ^gSomeone's laughing, ^dLord...

4. ^hSomeone's singing, ^dLord...

5. ⁱSomeone's praying, ^dLord...

6. ^aKum ba ^byah ^cmy ^dLord...

Actions:
a) roll hands   b) hands outstretched   c) point to self   d) point up   e) thumb and forefinger form circle   f) wipe eyes   g) forefingers to corners of mouth to show smile   h) cup hands around mouth   i) hands in praying position

Suggestions:

Make up additional verses such as:

    Someone's lonely, Lord, give him strength...
    Someone's fighting, Lord, give him peace...
    Someone's hating, Lord, give him love...
    Someone's doubting, Lord, give him faith...

THANK YOU

Thank you for the world so sweet,
Thank you for the food we eat,
Thank you for the birds that sing,
Thank you, God, for everything.

WHISPER A PRAYER

1. Whis-per a pray'r in the morn-ing, Whis-per a

pray'r at noon,——— Whis-per a pray'r in the

eve-ning, To keep—— your heart in tune.——

2. God answers pray'r in the morning,
   God answers pray'r at noon,
   God answers pray'r in the evening,
   He'll keep your heart in tune.

*Guitar play in key of E (E, A, B⁷)

GOD BLESS

God bless all those that I love,
God bless all those that love me,
God bless all those that love those that I love,
And all those that love those that love me.

GIVE ME OIL IN MY LAMP

A. Sevison

Give me oil in my lamp, Keep me

burn-ing, (burn-ing, burn-ing) Give me oil in my

lamp, I pray, (Hal-le-lu-ia) Give me oil in my

lamp, Keep me burn-ing, (burn-ing, burn-ing,)

Keep me burn-ing 'til the break of day.

Sing "Ho-san-na", sing "Ho-san-na,"

Sing "Ho-san-na to the King of Kings,"

Sing "Ho-san-na," sing "Ho-san-na,"

Sing "Ho-san-na to the King."——

Suggestion:

Divide into two groups. Group one sings verse and chorus without words in parentheses. Group two sings with group one on verse but adds words in parentheses. On chorus, group two sings descant of whole notes.

ISN'T HE WONDERFUL

Is-n't He won-der-ful, won-der-ful, won-der-ful,

Is-n't Je-sus, my Lord, won-der-ful! Eyes have

seen, ears have heard, It's re-cord-ed in God's

word. Is-n't Je-sus, my Lord, won-der-ful!

Actions:

a) clap in rhythm   b) hand shade eyes   c) hand cup ear   d) hands form book

39

STANDIN' IN THE NEED OF PRAYER

Spiritual

It's me, it's me, it's me, oh Lord,— stand-in' in the need of pray'r, Hal-le-lu-ia, It's me, it's me, it's me, oh Lord,— stand-in' in the need of pray'r.

1. Not my broth-er, not my sis-ter, but it's me, oh Lord,— stand-in' in the need of pray'r, Hal-le-lu-ia, Not my broth-er, not my sis-ter, but it's me, oh Lord,— stand-in' in the need of pray'r.

2. Not my mother, not my father, but it's me, oh Lord, ⟩ 2 times
   Standin' in the need of pray'r...
   Chorus

3. Not the preacher, not the deacon... Chorus

4. Not my neighbor, not a stranger... Chorus

40

HE'S GOT THE WHOLE WORLD

1. He's got the whole world – in His hands, He's got the whole world – in His hands, He's got the whole world – in His hands, He's got the whole world in His hands.

2. He's got the little, bitty baby in His hands,
   He's got the little, bitty baby in His hands,
   He's got the little, bitty baby in His hands,
   He's got the whole world in His hands.

3. He's got you and me brother...
4. He's got you and me sister...
5. He's got everybody here...
6. He's got the wind and the rain...
7. He's got the sun and the moon...
8. He's got the whole world...

DO LORD

Verse

1. I've got a home in glo-ry land that (clap) out-shines the sun, (Oh, Lord-y,) I've got a home in glo-ry land that (clap) out-shines the sun. I've got a home in glo-ry land that (clap) out-shines the sun, Look a-way be-yond—the blue.—

Chorus

Do Lord, oh, do Lord, oh, do re-mem-ber me, (Oh, Lord-y) Do Lord, oh, do Lord, oh, do re-mem-ber

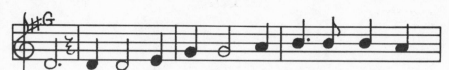
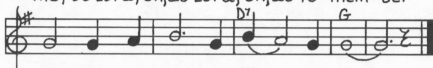

me, Do Lord, oh, do Lord, oh, do re-mem-ber

me, Look a-way be-yond — the blue.—

2. I took Jesus as my Savior,
   (clap) You take Him, too, (Oh, Lordy),
   I took Jesus as my Savior,
   (clap) You take Him, too,
   I took Jesus as my Savior,
   (clap) You take Him, too,
   Look away beyond the blue.
   Chorus

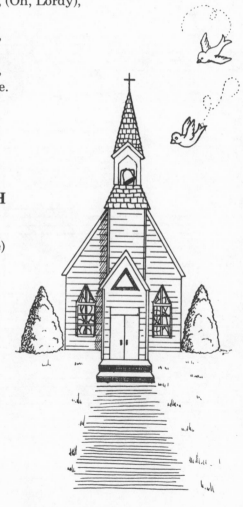

HERE IS THE CHURCH

Here is the church,
  (fold hands, fingers inside)
And here is the steeple,
  (index fingers up)
Open the doors,
  (thumbs apart)
And see all the people.
  (wiggle inside fingers)
Close the doors,
  (thumbs together)
And hear them pray,
  (hands to ear)
Open the doors,
  (thumbs apart)
And they all walk away.
  (fingers walk away)

43

CLIMB, CLIMB UP SUNSHINE MOUNTAIN

(a) Climb, climb up sun-shine moun-tain,

(b) Heav'n-ly breez-es blow, (a) Climb, climb up

sun-shine moun-tain, (c) Fac-es all a-glow,

(d) Turn, turn your face from doubt-ing,

(e) Look up in the sky, (a) Climb, climb up

sun-shine moun-tain, (f) you and (g) I.

Actions:
a) alternate hands as in climbing   b) wave hands from left to right   c) hands on
either side of face   d) look to right   e) look up   f) point out   g) point to self

44

HEAVENLY SUNSHINE

H.J. Zelley   *George H. Cooke*

Heav-en-ly sun-shine, heav-en-ly sun-shine,

Flood-ing my soul with glo-ry di-vine,——

Heav-en-ly sun-shine, heav-en-ly sun-shine,

Hal-le-lu-jah, Je-sus is mine.

PRAISE THE LORD TOGETHER
(Round)

Praise the Lord to-geth-er sing-ing,

"Al-le-lu-ia, al-le-lu-ia, al-le-lu-ia".

45

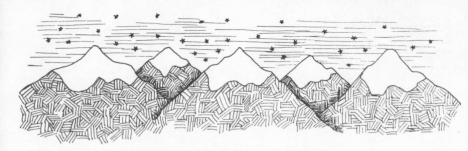

MY GOD IS SO GREAT

(a) My God is so great, so strong and so might-y! There's

(b) noth-ing my God can-not do! (clap, clap) My

(a) God is so great, so strong and so might-y! There's

(b) noth-ing my God can-not do! (clap, clap) The

(c) moun-tains are His, (d) the riv-ers are His, The

(e) stars are His hand-i-work too, —— My

*Guitar play in Key of E (E, A, B7)

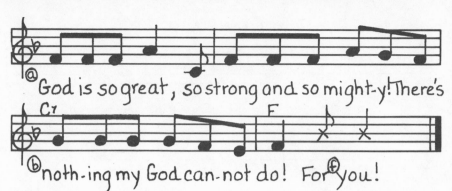

God is so great, so strong and so might-y! There's

noth-ing my God can-not do! For you!

Actions:
a) hold up arms and flex muscles   b) shake head "no"   c) hands form mountain
peak above head   d) wiggle fingers from left to right   e) fingers make twinkling
stars   f) point out

SEE THE CAMEL

See the camel, big and humpy,
(bend over, hands on knees)

See the elephant walk so clumpy,
(bend over, clasp hands and swing "trunk")

See the turtle, round and slow,
(squat down, make circle with arms in front of body)

God made them that way, you know.
(stand and point finger up)

See the squeaky mouse so small,
(crouch down, bend elbows, make little paws with hands)

Different from the horse that's tall,
(reach high on tiptoe)

See the robin flap his wings,
(flap arms)

Thank you, God, who made all things.
(bow head, fold hands in prayer)

47

PEACE LIKE A RIVER

1. I've got peace like a riv-er, I've got peace like a
riv-er, I've got peace like a riv-er in my soul.—
I've got peace like a riv-er, I've got peace like a
riv-er, I've got peace like a riv-er in my soul.—

2. I've got joy like a fountain...
3. I've got love like an ocean...

Optional Descant

I've got peace, — I've got peace, — I've got
peace — in my soul. — — I've got peace,—
I've got peace, — I've got peace — in my soul.—

48

WALKING WITH JESUS

*F   **B♭**   **C7**

Walk-ing with Je-sus, Walk-ing ev-'ry day,

F

All a-long the way, for I am walk-ing with

B♭   **C7**   **F**

Je-sus, Walk-ing with Je-sus a-lone.

Optional Descant

F   **B♭**

Walk-ing in the sun-light, Walk-ing in the sha-dow,

Suggestion:
Divide into two groups. Group one
sing song as written. Group two
sing descant where marked with
brackets. Join group one on
remaining measures.

* Guitar play in key of E (E, A, B7)

49

NOW I LAY

Now I lay me down to sleep,
 I pray the Lord my soul to keep,
Thy love be with me through the night,
 And keep me til the morning light.

FATHER, WE THANK THEE

Rebecca J. Weston   *Daniel Batchellor*

Fa-ther, we thank Thee for the — night,

And for the pleas-ant morn —ing— light,

For rest and food and lov-ing— care,

And all that makes the— world so —fair.

GOD IS SO GOOD

1. God is so good, God is so good,
God is so good, He's so good to me.

2. God loves me so, God loves me so,
   God loves me so, He's so good to me.
3. God answers prayer...

Optional Descant

S.N.

God — is so good to me, God — is so good,

God — is so good to me, so good to — me.

51

I'M IN THE LORD'S ARMY

(a) I may nev-er march in the in-fan-try,

(b) Ride in the cav-al-ry, (c) Shoot in the ar-til-ler-y,

(d) I may nev-er fly o'er the en-e-my, But

(e) I'm in the Lord's ar-my. (f) (yes sir!)

(e) I'm in the Lord's ar-my, (f) (yes sir!)

(e) I'm in the Lord's ar-my, (f) (yes sir!)

Actions:
a) march in place   b) hold reins, bounce as riding horse   c) clap once at shoulder
height, sliding one hand forward, one back   d) arms out as an airplane   e) hand to
brow in a salute   f) extend arm and return to salute in rhythm

HAPPY ALL THE TIME

I'm (a) in-right, (b) out-right, (c) up-right, (d) down-right

(e) hap-py all the time, I'm (a) in-right, (b) out-right,

(c) up-right, (d) down-right (e) hap-py all the time. Since

(f) Je-sus Christ came (g) in and (h) cleansed my

heart from sin, I'm (a) in-right, (b) out-right,

(c) up-right, (d) down-right (e) hap-py all the time.

Actions:
a) point to chest   b) point out   c) point up   d) point down   e) clap hands
f) arms up   g) point to chest with both hands   h) draw heart in air with both hands

GOD'S LOVE

Mauri Macy

Chorus

So I nev-er will for-get,— I sing a lit-tle song and this song al-ways re-minds me that God loves— me, And it's al-ways bet-ter yet—when some-one sings a-long— So two of us—can know a-bout—God's love.

Verse

1. He made pup-py dogs— pup-py dogs— to run and play with me and Kit-ty cats,— Kit-ty cats— as soft and warm can be,—

2. He made dairy cows, dairy cows to give us chocolate shakes,
   And dish rags, dish rags to clean the mess we make.   Chorus
3. He made sunshine, sunshine to warm the winter air,
   And woolly sheep, woolly sheep to give us clothes to wear. Chorus

54

Frederick Whitfield **OH, HOW I LOVE JESUS**

Oh, how I love Je - sus, Oh, how I love

Je - sus, — Oh, how I love Je - sus, be-

cause —— He first loved me. —

Part 2

To me, He is so won - der - ful and I

love — Him, To me, He is so won - der - ful and I

love — Him, To me, He is so won - der - ful and I

love — Him, be - cause — He first loved me.

*Guitar play in key of E (E, A, B⁷)

HALLELU, HALLELU

Hal-le-lu, hal-le-lu, hal-le-lu, hal-le-lu-jah!
Praise ye the Lord! Hal-le-lu, hal-le-lu, hal-le-lu, hal-le-lu-jah! Praise ye the Lord!
Praise ye the Lord, hal-le-lu-jah! Praise ye the Lord, hal-le-lu-jah! Praise ye the Lord, hal-le-lu-jah! Praise ye the Lord!

Suggestion:
Divide into two groups. Group 1 stand and sing on all the "Hallelus." Group 2 stand and sing on all the "Praise Ye the Lords." Sit when not singing.

OUR HANDS WE FOLD

Our hands we fold,
Our heads we bow,
For food and drink
We thank Thee now.

JESUS

1. Je—sus, Je—sus, Je-sus in the morn-ing, Je-sus at the noon-time, Je—sus, Je—sus, Je-sus when the sun goes down.

2. Praise Him, praise Him,
   Praise Him in the morning, praise Him at the noontime,
   Praise Him, praise Him,
   Praise Him when the sun goes down.

3. Love Him...

4. Serve Him...

5. Thank Him...

I LOVE TO TAKE A WALK

How I love to take a walk a-long the street,

And to say, "Hel-lo," to the peo-ple that I meet,

And to watch the show of their hap-py, hap-py feet,

And I say to my-self, It's a mir-a-cle.

Hal-le-lu, Hal—le-lu-ia! I sing as I walk a-

long, Hal-le-lu, Hal—le-lu-ia,

God has giv-en me such a hap-py, hap-py song,

THE WIND TELLS ME

The wind tells me,
   (sway like a tree in the wind)
The birds tell me,
   (flap arms)
The Bible tells me, too,
   (hands form book)
How much our Father loves us all,
   (arms outstretched)
And now I'm telling you.
   (point to self)   (point out)

RISE AND SHINE

Spiritual

Rise — and shine — and give God the glo-ry, glo-ry,

Rise — and shine — and give God the glo-ry, glo-ry,

Rise and shine and (clap) give God the glo-ry, glo-ry,

chil - dren of the Lord.

Actions:
a) hands in front, palms up and lift   b) hands outstretched on both sides of face
c) with hands still at sides of face, move upper body side to side in rhythm   d) clap in rhythm to end of phrase

DOWN IN MY HEART

George W. Cooke

1. I have the joy, joy, joy, joy down in my

heart, (where?) Down in my heart, (where?)

down in my heart, I have the joy, joy,

joy, joy down in my heart, (where?)

Down in my heart to stay. And I'm so

*Guitar play in key of A (A, D, E⁷)

60

hap-py, so ver-y hap-py, I have the love of

Je-sus in my heart, And I'm so hap-py, so ver-y

hap-py, I have the love of Je-sus in my heart.

2. I have the love of Jesus, love of Jesus down in my heart, (where?)
    Down in my heart, (where?) down in my heart,
    I have the love of Jesus, love of Jesus down in my heart, (where?)
    Down in my heart to stay.
        Chorus
3. I have the peace that passeth understanding...
        Chorus
4. I have the wonderful love of my blessed Redeemer way down in the
    depths of my heart...

REJOICE IN THE LORD ALWAYS

Philippians 4:4

(Round)

Re-joice in the Lord— al—ways and a-gain I

say re-joice! (clap!clap!) Re-joice in the Lord—

al— ways and a-gain I say re-joice! (clap,clap)

Re-joice,— re-joice,— and a-gain I say re-

joice! (clap,clap) Re-joice,— re-joice,— and a-

gain I say re-joice! (clap, clap)

INDEX

*Titles with asterisks are fingerplays which are rhymes illustrated by the use of finger motions.